£5

Live Steam

1

1   The SVR has a good selection of Moguls, and here, one of
them, Ivatt class 4 2-6-0 No. 43106, is departing from
Bridgnorth on Saturday, 5 April 1975, with a morning train for
Bewdley. (DE)

DAVID EATWELL and
JOHN H. COOPER-SMITH

Live Steam

Locomotives and lines today

B. T. Batsford Ltd, *London*

First published 1980
© David Eatwell and John H. Cooper-Smith 1980

ISBN 0 7134 2079 0

Printed in Great Britain by
The Anchor Press Ltd, Tiptree, Essex
for the publishers B T Batsford Ltd
4 Fitzhardinge Street, London W1H 0AH

Contents

Acknowledgment
The authors of this album could not possibly have
achieved such wide coverage and so many diverse
photographic locations without the willing co-
operation and assistance of large numbers of people
on the railways concerned, and this is most thankfully
acknowledged here. In addition, the advice and
constructive criticism by many expert friends during
the preparation of the volume has also been most
gratefully received, and in this connection, particular
thanks must be given to John Morse, David ('Wilf')
McClelland, Robin Waywell, Murray Brown, Chris
Williams, Mike Esau, David Williams and John
Titlow.

Introduction

We British, it seems, have always loved our railways . . . after all, we *did* invent them! . . . and in particular, we have, often passionately, loved our locomotives, at least since the days of the 'railway mania' back in the last century when the smooth lines and latent power of those hissing monsters began to be noticed by an ever increasing number of admirers whenever they took to the rails.

As the railway network spread throughout the country, more and more locomotives were needed to work it, and as all the railways were privately owned, each separate company had to set about the task of providing the locomotives for the job; the bigger companies having workshops for the purpose. In this way, many hundreds of different locomotive types emerged, since each Chief Mechanical Engineer had his own ideas on design, and built the locomotives to suit his requirements, whilst the many private builders were doing the same for those lines unable (or unwilling) to produce their own motive power. New designs quickly followed earlier ones, the majority of which have unfortunately not survived, but occasionally the odd example or two escaped extinction for one reason or another until, when eventually these veterans of the track really *were* time-expired, someone somewhere, realised that perhaps future generations might like to see machines which had been built way back near the very birth of the railways, and some were preserved.

The earliest of these, *Wylam Dilly* of 1813, is in the Royal Scottish Museum, Edinburgh, and other early 'wonders' are at York and Darlington, whilst the most famous of all, Stephenson's *Rocket* is in the Science Museum in London along with another 1829 locomotive, *Sanspareil.* These static exhibits, 'stuffed and mounted' on lengths of track little longer than the locomotives themselves, are not, generally speaking, meant to be used any more, but recently there has been a move to construct full-sized replicas of some of our more important relics, and these duplicates actually steam! A modern reconstruction of George Stephenson's 1825 *Locomotion No. 1* led the cavalcade of famous locomotives at Shildon in 1975, and more recently copies of *Rocket, Sanspareil* and *Novelty* have all been constructed from the original drawings for the re-enactment, in 1980, of the Rainhill Trials. Who'd have thought, when British

Rail banned steam from its lines in 1968, that newly constructed steam locomotives would be running along them some dozen or so years later?

But such show-cases are, by their very nature, something of a rarity, and it is to our privately run railways that we must go if we are to see regular steam-hauled trains today, and to the steam-centres if we are to see those locomotives which British Rail have had second thoughts about and which now *are* allowed on their metals . . . sometimes. Not all of them are always accessible to visitors, but where trains do run, this is made perfectly clear in the published time-tables, and Open Days at the steam-centres are almost invariably advertised well in advance giving visitors the opportunity to sample the nostalgic delights of a steam-hauled ride. Many dozens of such locations exist throughout the mainland of Britain, and we, the authors, have done our best to use as wide a selection of our photographs as we can in this volume. It will be seen, however, that to include pictures of every railway or even of every class of locomotive that has been preserved is impossible, so to those whose lines or locomotives have been omitted we offer our sincere apologies. In mitigation, perhaps, we might just mention that our intentions have not been to be comprehensive, merely representative. In our chapter headings and selection an inclusion or omission here is in no way an indication of importance, or lack of it!

A particular aim has, however, been to include specimens of as many different types of the steam locomotives working in this country as we can (excluding industrials), irrespective of their gauge (down to 15 inches) or country of origin, and *without* being drawn in to the controversy over the meaning of the word 'preserved'! Thus, we show pictures of the Vale of Rheidol Railway and the Romney, Hythe & Dymchurch Railway, for example, as well as *Flying Scotsman* (purchased from British Rail in working order), *King Haakon 7* (brought over from Norway in working order), and *Greene King* (rescued as a rusting hulk from Barry scrapyard and subsequently completely restored), thereby embracing all these, and many other, forms of pleasure steam-railways within the general term 'preservation'.

In our previous volume *Return to Steam*, we dealt with steam on British Rail since the 1968 'ban',

whilst here we concentrate on the other side of the preservation movement, the non-BR lines. In most cases though, these belonged to British Rail until that organisation decided to give them up as uneconomic, and they were taken over and re-opened by private groups and individuals who turned them into the highly successful ventures that we know today. Each attracts an ever increasing number of annual visitors, and the published accounts usually show a continually healthy position, and deservedly so. This is in no small way due to the dedication and sheer professionalism of the staff. That these locomotives are working at all is often something of a minor miracle as spare parts become more and more difficult to obtain, and it can even be necessary to have some made 'one-off' abroad, and at enormous expense, too. The expertise of some of our top engineers must also be acknowledged, for without their know-how, the tasks of restoration and maintenance would surely be impossible. The lover of steam locomotives today owes a debt of gratitude to all those workers, mainly unpaid volunteers, who give up their time and get their hands dirty in order to keep the wheels turning so that the tens of thousands of visitors who make the journey each year for a 'whiff of steam' or a 'ride in the past' shall not be disappointed. We thank them all, very, very much.

DAVID EATWELL, JOHN H. COOPER–SMITH

1980

The Severn Valley Railway

The SVR began as a project to preserve the line between Bridgnorth and Hampton Loade which is part of the old route from Worcester to Shrewsbury, closed in the Beeching era. After a successful start, the next section was opened to Bewdley, and, more recently, to Foley Park, bringing the line to within a couple of miles or so of Kidderminster. The track to this point is still in situ, providing a connection with BR which enables SVR locomotives and rolling stock to operate on the main line. The society and its motive power is strongly flavoured with the GWR with a noticeable LMS filling – a position much in keeping with its geographical situation and operation before preservation. For the photographer, the SVR offers a good selection of vantage points, and adds to the appeal with its steam locomotives which are maintained to a very high standard, and with its fleet of coaching stock, run in rakes in uniform liveries, although some diesels have recently been noted along the route.

2 On the afternoon of Saturday, 5 April 1975, Ivatt Mogul No. 46521 2-6-0 (this one of class 2) is seen from across the River Severn as it nears Bewdley with one of the last trains of the day from Bridgnorth. (DE)

3 Stanier class 5 4-6-0 No. 45110 pulls out of Eardington station with a rake of LMS coaches, a scene which could easily have been fifteen years earlier than the day this photograph was taken: 27 September 1975. (JHCS)

4

4 GWR 2-6-2T No. 4566 with three matching GWR coaches form the early spring service in 1976 as they accelerate away from the slack over the Severn on their way to Bewdley, and later . . .

5 . . . return to Bridgnorth on the Victoria Bridge. The date is 6 March. (JHCS)

6 Regarded by many as one of the least lovely of our preserved locomotives, No. 600 *Gordon* is a wartime built 2-10-0, and in its bright livery of red and blue contrasts vividly with the grey stone buildings of Highley station as it pulls away with a southbound Enthusiasts' Special on Sunday, 17 April 1977. (DE)

5

6

8

7 Making its first appearance on a public train this weekend, BR Standard class 4 2-6-4T No. 80079 – not fully lined out yet – works a northbound train past Trimpley Reservoir on the afternoon of Sunday, 17 April 1977. (DE)

8 The SVR's 'Jinty' 0-6-0T No. 47383 is serviced between round trips at Bridgnorth on Saturday, 15 April 1978; taking water, and . . .

9 . . . having a meal of coal offered to the bunker. (JHCS)

9

10 With the lining-out now complete, the Standard class 4 Tank crosses the Eardington-Highley road at the head of an evening train for Bridgnorth during an Enthusiasts' Weekend of intensive train services, 15 April 1978. (JHCS)

11 Built at Crewe in 1950, 2-6-0 No. 6443 is nevertheless an LMS design, and on Sunday afternoon, 16 April 1978, it heads south past Trimpley Reservoir with a train for Bewdley. (DE)

12 The classic lines of one of Stanier's 'masterpieces of design' are exemplified in this view of 2-8-0 8F No. 8233 as it effortlessly hauls its five-coach load past Trimpley Reservoir on its way to Bewdley on Sunday, 16 April 1978. (DE)

13 One of the most numerous classes of preserved steam locomotive is the 0-6-0T 'Austerity', there being at least two dozen at present, and this number is increasing all the time as more and more are replaced by diesels by the NCB and other industrial organisations. The LNER had 75 of them as their class J94, and this title is generally used when refering to any one of them, even though it was probably not an ex-LNER locomotive. Various builders supplied them (Hudswell Clarke, Robert Stephenson and Hawthorn, Andrew Barclay), and this

one is No. 193, a Hunslet built in 1953, shown here with sailing going on in the background on Trimpley Reservoir during the afternoon of Sunday, 16 April 1978, heading north. (DE)

14 On the occasion of its re-naming ceremony by the designer, R. A. Riddles, Esq. (who also designed the 'Austerity' above), *Britannia* is steamed at Bridgnorth on the morning of Saturday, 20 May 1978. In April 1980, it moved to Wansford. (JHCS)

15 Ever mindful of the joys of simply watching the trains go by, the SVR occasionally holds special events for enthusiasts when trains run over the little-used section to Foley Park, south of Bewdley, as well as the 'main-line' to Bridgnorth. Just such a day is Sunday, 10 September 1978, when 4-6-0 *Hinton Manor* sets out in the morning sunshine, and . . .

16 . . . newly restored Pacific *Britannia* does the same thing in the afternoon. (DE)

17 On Sunday, 22 April 1979, Black Five 4-6-0 No. 45000 undergoes a steam-test in the shed at Bridgnorth; *Raveningham Hall* awaiting a turn of duty alongside. (DE)

18 Built at Swindon in 1929, 0-6-0 Pannier Tank No. 5764 (and a rake of LMS coaches) heads for Bridgnorth on the evening of Sunday, 22 April 1979. (DE)

15

16

7

8

The Keighley and Worth Valley Railway

The Worth Valley line was the first standard gauge line to be re-opened in the period when steam was vanishing from British Rail service in a big way, in 1968 when enthusiasm for preservation was at a very high level. Running from Keighley to Oxenhope, a distance of five miles or so, the trains have a steep climb all the way up the Worth Valley. There is a connection with British Rail at the northern end, used by the K&WVR for transferring locomotives between themselves and the National Railway Museum, for example, and for running 'through' trains from various points in Britain to Oxenhope, steam hauled on their line. A great asset in photographic terms is the combination of excellent vantage points and the stiff gradient, recognised by film-makers in the production of classics such as 'The Railway Children' and, more recently, 'Yanks'. This photographic potential was also recognised by the late Bishop Eric Treacy, railway photographer par excellence, and the line's president for many years.

19 All guts and thunder at Haworth yard as 0-6-0ST *Fred* and 2-6-4T No. 80002 struggle for adhesion with the morning empty-stock train to Oxenhope on 21 April 1973. (JHCS)

20 2-6-4T No. 80002 makes its way from Haworth to Oxenhope through the woods with a midday train on 21 April 1973. (JHCS)

21

22

21 Early morning line-up. At about 08.00hrs on Sunday, 1 July 1973, three locomotives raise steam in Haworth yard, ready to work the day's tourist trains between Keighley and Oxenhope. On the left is an Ivatt 2-6-2T of 1949, in the centre is a GWR 0-6-0 Pannier Tank of 1929, and on the right, *Fred*, one of the Austerity 0-6-0 Saddle Tanks stabled at Haworth, this one dating from 1945. Later in the morning . . .

22 . . . the Pannier Tank crosses Mytholmes Viaduct with a southbound train, whilst . . .

23 . . . during the afternoon, the Ivatt Tank makes a brisk re-start from Damens Halt with another train from Keighley. (DE)

24 On Enthusiasts' Day 1974 (30 March), under the watchful eye of Chris Williams the rare phenomenon of the steaming of the Lancashire and Yorkshire 0-4-0ST took place. The 1901 locomotive, one of a class of dock-shunters nicknamed 'Pugs', does not, however, often venture out of Haworth yard where this shot was taken. (JHCS)

23

24

25

25 and 26 On another of the Worth Valley Enthusiasts' Days,
Saturday, 22 March 1975, a rare combination of spring
sunshine and steam is seen when the Lancashire and Yorkshire
Railway's Barton Wright 0-6-0 No. 52044 of 1887 pilots
0-6-0ST Austerity *Brussels* on one of the afternoon trains out of
Keighley. (JHCS)

27 *Evening Star,* a great favourite during its stay on the line, emerges from Ingrow Tunnel with an afternoon train for Oxenhope on Saturday, 22 March 1975 . . .

28 . . . and a few weeks later in April, crosses Mytholmes Viaduct in the spring sunshine. (JHCS)

27

28

29 Ex-Swedish Railways 2-8-0 No. 1931, caught by the camera leaving Keighley on Sunday, 27 April 1975, has the same design of chassis, front end and boiler as the British WD 2-8-0 locomotives, but the cab and tender differ. It is, however, the nearest we shall ever see to a preserved 2-8-0 WD as no British example survives from the 733 locomotives built. (JHCS)

30 Stanier class 5 4-6-0 No. 45212 pounds out of Keighley on 10 September 1975. (JHCS)

30

27

31

31 The Worth Valley Railway was the first line to run Santa Specials on the weekends before Christmas, the trains running from Damens Sidings or Oakworth to Oxenhope, and being usually double-headed. On Sunday, 14 December 1975, Stanier 8F No. 8431 and the Swedish 2-8-0 blast out of Oakworth in the morning sunshine, whilst . . .

32 . . . later in the day, the same pair are caught in a similar position, the sun having obligingly provided the camera with an alternative viewpoint. (JHCS)

28

33 No. 3924 was built at Derby for the Midland Railway in 1920, and was rescued from the scrapyard in 1968 by the Midland 4F Preservation Society which has restored it to the earliest BR style with the words 'British Railways' in full on the tender, and 40,000 added to the MR number. On Enthusiasts' Day, Sunday, 28 March 1976, the 0-6-0 explodes out of Ingrow Tunnel with a morning train from Keighley, and . . .

34 . . . later on the same day, pilots the 8F No. 8431 through the cutting out of Mytholmes Tunnel with a train for Oxenhope. (JHCS)

35 The first train of the day deposits passengers at Oxenhope, the locomotive being a BR Standard class 4 4-6-0 from the early fifties and the date is 11 September 1977 . . . (DE)

36 . . .whilst exactly a week later, the same locomotive attacks the slope between Damens and Oakworth with gusto as it heads a Sunday morning train from Keighley . . .

37 . . . and that evening, it returns to Haworth with the last train of the day. (JHCS)

38 On temporary loan from the National Railway Museum, GNR atlantic No. 990 *Henry Oakley* double-heads an 0-6-0ST out of Oakworth on Enthusiasts' Day in March 1978. (JHCS)

39 For several years West Country class pacific No. 34092 *City of Wells* has been under restoration out in the open at Haworth, but the immense task of converting 86 tons of rusting steel (not to mention the tender!) to a gleaming, working machine is an understandably long job. As this book closed for press, the job had just been completed, and the loco returned to service. The date of this picture is March 1978. (JHCS)

40 The Worth Valley Railway sometimes runs freight trains for the benefit of those who attend Enthusiasts' Days, and that in March 1978 sees the Standard class 4 leaving Keighley on such a working. (JHCS)

41 The Father Christmas specials are always a popular feature with young and old alike (the children get their presents and their parents get their punch!), and this one has the added bonus of a pair of American locomotives hauling it. In front is No. 5828, an Sl60 class 2-8-0 (nicknamed 'Big Jim,' and arriving here via Poland), followed by No. 72, an 0-6-0T, both working very hard up the grade out of Haworth and heading for Oxenhope on the afternoon of Sunday, 17 December 1978. (DE)

40

41

The North Yorkshire Moors Railway

It seems incredible that the North Yorkshire Moors Railway, a line which one would have said had always been with us, did not in fact celebrate its fifth anniversary until 1978, so important a feature of the British steam scene is it. But the official opening ceremony was performed by HRH the Duchess of Kent on 1 May 1973, although members had in fact been able to travel for some time prior to this date, and the locomotives there had been steamed and run on test trips and galas since the beginning of the decade. The superb photographic locations and wide variety of locomotive stock make the NYMR, with its steeply graded route, one of the most popular lines in Britain to the steam enthusiast. From Grosmont to Goathland, the line rises steeply at 1 in 49, followed by a descent from Eller Beck through Newton Dale to Pickering, making a journey of some eighteen miles or so. What was for some time a 100 per cent steam railway has unfortunately of recent years been used for the running of diesel-hauled trains, but those services which *are* steam-hauled offer some of the most spectacular sights and sounds to be found anywhere in Britain. Two locomotives, Kl 2-6-0 No. 2005 and Black Five No. 4767 *George Stephenson* are passed for running on British Rail and can gain access to the national system at Grosmont.

42

42 Known as a 'Lambton Tank' after the colliery in which it used to work, No. 29 is an 0-6-2T built by Kitson and dating from 1904. It can usually be relied upon to provide the photographer with a spectacular smoke display, such as on this Easter Saturday in 1973, while it thrashes up the 1 in 49 at Beck Hole with a special train for Goathland. (DE)

43 On Sunday, 8 June 1975, a special train runs over the newly re-opened line from Goathland southwards to Pickering, consisting of ten coaches double-headed by Black Five 4-6-0 No. 5428 and K1 2-6-0 No. 2005. The pair are negotiating the curves in Newton Dale on the descent to the 'new' southern terminus. (JHCS)

43

44 The GNR J52 0-6-0ST No. 1247 crosses Water Arc with a southbound train on Sunday, 22 June 1975, during the climb up to Goathland . . .

45 . . . and later in the day, bursts out from under Beck Hole bridge. The loco has since been donated to the National Railway Museum. (JHCS)

46 Darnholme is one of the many picturesque spots on the NYMR, and Black Five No. 5428 makes a majestic sight as it climbs up towards Goathland with an evening train on Sunday, 3 August 1975. (DE)

45

46

47

49

47 The first train of the day on Saturday, 20 September 1975, emerges from the tunnel at Grosmont behind Black Five *Eric Treacy*. (JHCS)

48 With a nip in the air on a beautiful autumn morning of the last day in October 1975, the K1 blasts up the 1 in 49 between Esk Cottages and Beck Hole with one of the Gala Day trains, and . . .

49 . . . amongst other locomotives in steam are the two North Eastern mineral engines; left, Q6 0-8-0 (ex-BR No. 63395) in NER livery as T2 class No. 2238, overtaking J27 (ex-BR No. 65894) also in NER livery as P3 0-6-0 No. 2392 at the mouth of Grosmont Tunnel. Both locomotives are on view later in the day . . .

50 . . . as the T2 continues its journey to Pickering past the splendid NER signal gantry at Goathland, and . . .

48

51 ... the P3 hauls a special freight near Beck Hole. (JHCS)

51

52 Sporting the star from the Silksworth Colliery Branch, the 0-6-2 Lambton Tank makes hard work of lifting the 3-coach Santa Special along the wet and slippery rails, and up the difficult incline past Esk Cottages on Sunday, 12 December 1976. (DE)

53 Although shortly to go to the National Railway Museum at York, the P3 had a good deal of use on passenger trains, here exemplified by the 16.00hrs train to Goathland, leaving Grosmont on May Day, 1977. (JHCS)

54

54 Viewed from the road near Fylingdales, class 5 No. 4767 *George Stephenson* heads back to Grosmont with an afternoon train from Pickering on Sunday, 1 May 1977. (DE)

55 Approaching Eller Beck summit with a morning northbound train also on Sunday, 1 May 1977, is the unique Stephenson Link Black Five which, . . .

7

56 . . . in the afternoon does another round trip to Pickering, being photographed leaving Levisham . . . (JHCS)

57 . . . and passing up through Newton Dale. (DE)

58 Transformed in appearance by the addition of 'blinkers' (added, for some obscure reason, during the filming of a recent cigar commercial), *George Stephenson* works hard with a light load near Beck Hole on the first train on Gala Day, Sunday, 23 April 1978. (DE)

58

59

59 The second Lambton Tank on the NYMR is No. 5, and although it is similar in appearance to No. 29, it was in fact constructed by a different builder . . . Stephenson . . . and despite its lower number, five years *later* in 1909. Gala Day, Sunday, 23 April 1978, sees it coasting down past the disused Newton Dale signal box during the afternoon with a packed train from Grosmont to Pickering, whilst . . . (DE)

60 . . . later in the day, and sporting the royal crest to commemorate the fifth anniversary of the re-opening of the line, the K1 No. 2005 catches the spring sunshine under Darnholme bridge during its journey south. (JHCS)

The Bluebell Railway

61 LBSCR 0-6-2T No. 473 *Birch Grove* of 1898 puffs through the woods near Freshfield Halt on 5 April 1969 and . . .

62 . . . in between turns, shunts some of the SECR Birdcage stock at Horsted Keynes. (JHCS)

The first preserved standard-gauge line was the Bluebell, being conceived as long ago as 1959, a far-sighted move although at that time it was seen mainly as a means of preserving some of the small pre-grouping classes of locomotive which were then rapidly disappearing. However, in recent years a policy of including larger engines has been pursued, bearing in mind the possibility of expanding the line to East Grinstead. At present, the Bluebell operates over only about five miles of track, but this runs through some very pretty Sussex countryside between Sheffield Park and Horsted Keynes, which produces very suitable backgrounds for the photography of the Southern locomotives being used, especially when they are run in conjunction with the fleet of authentic coaching stock from the same period. The comprehensively equipped workshops, combined with full-time engineers, and seemingly limitless enthusiasm, ensure that both locomotives and coaching stock are maintained in top condition, as indeed they have to be to pass the stringent tests imposed by the authorities before permission to carry members of the public is granted.

62

63 On 17 June 1969 the biggest working loco on the line was the GWR Dukedog 4-4-0 No. 3217 *Earl of Berkeley* which here accelerates out of Sheffield Park into the afternoon sunshine, and with the last train of the day, . . .

64 . . . is seen in semi-silhouette as that same sun sets in the evening. (JHCS)

65 Also on 17 June 1969 the oldest working ex-BR locomotive, A1X 0-6-0T No. 72 *Fenchurch* does quite well for a centenarian as it maintains a stately 15mph with its 3-coach train near Horsted Keynes waterworks. (JHCS)

63

67

66 One of four such locomotives preserved in this country (two are on the Kent & East Sussex Railway, and one on the Keighley and Worth Valley Railway), No. 30064 was built by Vulcan Ironworks USA in 1943 for use overseas, and was eventually purchased with thirteen others by the SR for work in Southampton Docks. Here it is at Horsted Keynes on 22 July 1973 having just brought up a Sunday afternoon train from Sheffield Park, and moving past the new carriage-shed on its way to rejoin its train for the return journey. (DE)

67 BR Standard class 4 4-6-0 No. 75027 was built at Swindon in 1952 and came to the Bluebell Railway after withdrawal from BR in 1968. On Sunday, 22 July 1973, it pulls a fairly full train up the 1 in 75 of Freshfield Bank, lit by the long low rays of the evening sun. (DE)

68 On 10 November 1974 P class 0-6-0T No. 27 of 1909 pulls away from Sheffield Park with the 12.45hrs train for Horsted Keynes. (DE)

69 Built in 1885 by Neilson of Glasgow, No. 488 was one of a class of 71 locomotives designed by Adams of the LSWR to work the Waterloo suburban services round about the turn of the century, but were displaced by the electrification in 1915, and withdrawal started the following year. However, No. 488 was one of a trio of this 0415 class locomotive which, for varying reasons, worked the Lyme Regis Branch until 1961, and was subsequently acquired by the Bluebell Railway. Here it shunts the Great Northern Railway Directors' Saloon at Horsted Keynes on Saturday, 6 December 1975. (DE)

68

69

71

70 The pride of the line today is undoubtedly the Bulleid Pacific No. 21C123 *Blackmore Vale* which has been restored at Sheffield Park to the highest standards, and on the occasion of its entry into traffic, a typical formation of Bulleid stock was used to form an 'Atlantic Coast Express', complete with head- and roofboards. This scene could easily have been on the fringes of Dartmoor in 1947/8, but is in fact at Holywell on Saturday, 15 May 1976. Surely railway preservation at its very best. (JHCS)

71 The Wainwright class C 0-6-0 of 1901 has its fire thrown at Sheffield Park in the evening of Wednesday, 22 June 1977, after bringing in the last train of the day from Horsted Keynes some 15 or 20 minutes earlier. On the left is the U class mogul of 1928, having arrived from Tenterden (K&ESR) only a few days previously. (DE)

72 The last train of the evening heads for Horsted Keynes behind the Brighton-built 2-6-0 U class locomotive on Sunday, 11 September 1977. (JHCS)

72

73

73 This 0-4-4T by Wainwright was built at Ashford in 1905 as one of the H class of suburban tank locomotives, and on withdrawal from service by BR in 1964, came via Ashford to Sheffield Park where, on Sunday, 10 December 1978, it sits sedately in the station ready to depart with a morning train for Horsted Keynes. (DE)

74 Two locomotives in Sheffield Park Works on Sunday, 8 April 1979 are: *top* BR class 4 4-6-0 No. 75027, and *bottom* minus its boiler, A1X 'Terrier' class 0-6-0T *Fenchurch*. (See pics Nos. 67 and 65.) (DE)

75 Three locomotives awaiting restoration in the yard at Sheffield Park on Sunday, 8 April 1979 are, L to R, 9F 2-10-0 No. 92240, Maunsell Q class 0-6-0 No. 30541, and *Baxter,* an 0-4-0T industrial locomotive built by Fletcher Jennings & Co in 1877. (DE)

Some Narrow Gauge Lines

Just as the word 'preserved' is open to more than one interpretation, so too is the expression 'Narrow Gauge', and again we must decline from accepting a hard and fast definition of the term. Instead, we will say that all the pictures in this section depict locomotives which run on rails less than the Standard Gauge of 4 feet 8½ inches, but not less than 15 inches because anything smaller than the latter size tends to be regarded as either 'miniature' or 'model', and is really outside the general theme of this book. As is so often the case, it has proved quite impossible to do any real justice to the Narrow Gauge scene as a whole, simply because of its sheer size and scope, but we *have* included more than a dozen different lines, with over twice this number of locomotives, and hope that these will give the reader some idea of the charm and delights to be found along the little lines in rural Britain.

76

76 The Ravenglass & Eskdale Railway is a 15 inch line in the Lake District, running inland from the coast in especially scenic surroundings, and *Northern Rock* is their newest locomotive, here passing Muncaster Mill on the way back to Ravenglass on Easter Sunday, 1978. One of the earlier locomotives, . . .

77 *River Esk*, hauls a full train near the same site on Tuesday, 4 July also in 1978. For a few years prior to this date, Standard Gauge steam-hauled trains have run along the Cumbrian coast, making a stop at Ravenglass to allow passengers the opportunity of further steam haulage on the NG line to Dalegarth, and this is one of the trains so employed, absolutely bristling with travellers. No doubt, so long as 'The Cumbrian Coast Express' runs from Carnforth to Sellafield, the R&E will be in the happy position of being able to augment the facilities offered in this manner. (DE)

78 At the opposite end of England to the Ravenglass &
Eskdale Railway is the only other major 15inch line in the
country, the Romney, Hythe & Dymchurch Railway which,
despite its name, runs between Hythe and Dungeness! The
main shed and 'centre' of the line is at New Romney, and on
Sunday, 13 June 1976, three of the four locomotives in steam,
Dr Syn (left), *Hurricane* (centre) and *Typhoon* are together here
at about noon. The fourth locomotive, *Winston Churchill*, brings
in a lengthy train to Dungeness at about 15.00hrs . . .

79 . . . as viewed from the top of the old lighthouse. (DE)

80 A year later, *Black Prince*, the Krupp-built Pacific, poses on
the New Romney turntable between trips on the afternoon of
22 June. (DE)

78

81

81 In its heyday, slate-quarrying in the mountains of Wales was a particularly thriving industry, and Narrow Gauge railways were often used to transport the product down to the coast for shipment. The actual gauge of each railway seemed to be a matter of personal choice, but the majority were in the region of 1 foot 10½ inches to 2 feet, and a most interesting selection of locomotives has survived. *Maid Marian* was built by Hunslet in 1903, and came here to Bala Lake from Dinorwic via Bressingham and Llanberis, and on a very wet and misty Sunday afternoon, 10 September 1978, trundles along in fine form. (DE)

82 *Gwynedd,* shown at Bressingham on Sunday, 4 July 1971, is another Hunslet, built for the Penrhyn system in 1883, and, seen on the same afternoon is . . .

83 *Bronwllyd,* also from Penrhyn, but of only 1930 vintage, and a Hudswell Clarke. This locomotive is really a hybrid, since it was completely rebuilt here at Bressingham under the direction of the owner, Mr Alan Bloom, who is actually at the controls of this unique machine. (DE)

84

84 The Festiniog Railway runs up into the hills from the coastal town of Porthmadog, and of recent years has been heavily involved in building a lengthy deviation at the upper end to skirt an electricity board reservoir which flooded a long section of the original route. Narrow Gauge steam is once more to be seen near Blaenau Ffestiniog, and among the locomotive stock are some of the strangest looking machines one would see in many a long day, such as the Double Fairlies built in the railway's own workshops at Boston Lodge. On Saturday, 17 December 1977, *Merddyn Emrys,* the 1879 0-4-4-0T emerges from its shed in a cloud of steam, ready to haul a Santa Special up to the temporary terminus at Llyn Ystradau, and . . .

85 . . . approaching Penrhyn during the climb. Many other locomotives are here, . . .

86 . . . including one of a small handful of American locomotives in Britain, this 1916-built import, constructed by Alco, and previously used in France. (DE)

87 Many of the stately homes of England have achieved much in the field of steam preservation by installing railways in their grounds, and typical of them is Knebworth, near Stevenage in Hertfordshire, which on occasion invites other locomotives to visit the line for special events. Such an occasion was on Saturday, 24 July 1976, when the Rev. Teddy Boston brought his 1919 Bagnall 0-4-0ST *Pixie* from the rectory at Cadeby (he is seen here on the footplate with some young friends) to join *Sezela No. 4* (right), a 1916 Avonside from Natal. The largest locomotive on view, . . .

88 . . . No. 99.3461, is one of only three or four East German locomotives ever seen in this country, having been built in Stettin in 1925, and having spent some time in the car park at New Romney on the RH&DR before working here and then going abroad again. (DE)

89 BR's only steam-operated line is from Aberystwyth to Devil's Bridge, and the three 2-6-2T locomotives which work all the services date back to a design of 1902. There are no turning facilities, so 'down' trains are hauled bunker first, like this one leaving the upper terminus at about 16.15hrs on Sunday, 16 July 1972. In 1978, a programme of replacing the original coal fuel with a system of oil-firing, similar to that used on the Festiniog and other railways, was introduced, and somehow this seems to rob the locomotives of some of their romance. On Good Friday, 24 March of that year, No. 9, *Prince of Wales* had not been so modified as it nears the end of the line . . .

90 . . . still looking and sounding as spectacular as ever, on its 1 foot 11½ inch gauge rails. (DE)

91 The Leighton Buzzard Narrow Gauge Railway runs from Stonehenge (Bedfordshire, not Wiltshire!) to Pages Park along the 2 foot gauge rails of a former sand-quarry line, and uses some interesting steam locomotives amongst the diesels which seem to haul so many of their weekend passenger trains. *Pixie*, a 1922 Kerr Stuart, runs into Pages Park with a Sunday afternoon train on 26 September 1971, and . . .

92 *Chaloner*, a centenarian 0-4-0 vertical boiler Tank by de Winton and Chaplin, came from the Pen-y-Orsedd quarries to Leighton Buzzard where it has been completely overhauled by its owner, Mr Alf Fisher. He and his son David are, unusually, together on the footplate on Saturday, 16 July 1977, as it hauls empty-coaching stock (the passengers are staff, and an important duty is to extinguish fires between the rails!) towards Pages Park for one of its rare public outings prior to being put on display in the National Railway Museum, York, during 1979. (DE)

91

92

93 Built by SFB Raimes in occupied France in 1944, this
0-8-0T ran on various 2 foot 6 inch (760mm) continental lines
before being brought over to the Welshpool and Llanfair Light
Railway in 1969 to help out a motive-power shortage at that
time. It arrived from the Steirmarkische Landesbahn in Austria
as their No. 699.01, but was soon given the number 10 and the
name *Sir Drefaldwyn*. On Sunday, 30 April 1972, it works
alongside the picturesque River Banwy, hauling a rake of
balcony coaches, recently arrived from the Zillertalbahn.
Returning to Britain after spending much of its previous life in
Sierra Leone is . . .

93

94

94 W&LLR No. 14, a Hunslet 2-6-2T of 1954 which now
returns a Good Friday afternoon train to Llanfair on 13 April
1979.

95 For some obscure reason, when the Tal-y-Llyn Railway was built in 1886, it was laid to 2 foot 3 inch gauge, not unique, just unusual, and especially so since the neighbouring Festiniog Railway had already come into operation using 1 foot 11½ inch rails, and one would have supposed uniformity would have been encouraged! Under private ownership, the locomotive stock was increased by the acquisition of, among others, an ex-Corris Railway 0-6-0ST, built by Falcon Engineering (now Brush) in 1878, and subsequently named *Sir Haydn* in honour of the former general manager and local MP Sir Haydn Jones. On Saturday, 31 March 1969, this venerable locomotive sits simmering at the Wharf Station, Tywyn, ready to haul its train up some 1 in 45 gradients to the upper terminus at Abergynolwyn, some seven miles distant. (DE)

96 In the shadow of Cader Idris, and just south of the Mawddach Estuary, is the small village of Fairbourne, home of a two-mile-long 15 inch gauge railway, and a truly magnificent stud of locomotives, including an Atlantic from 1909 and a Pacific from 1949. An important source of income to this, the Fairbourne Railway, is the carriage of passengers to and from the Barmouth cross-estuary ferry, but these are by no means the only people who visit this part of the Welsh coast for a ride through the sand dunes behind steam, as both local holiday-makers and enthusiasts come in sufficient numbers to keep this lovely little line (no longer called the Fairbourne *Miniature* Railway), deservedly busy throughout the summer months.

On Wednesday, 1 August 1979, there was a line-up of locomotives at Fairbourne station, and these were, from L to R, *Ernest W. Twining* (a Guest-built Pacific of 1949), *Katie* (another Guest-built locomotive, but this one a 2-4-2 of 1954—sister loco *Sian* was out on a train) and *Count Louis* (a Bassett Lowke 4-4-2 of 1909). (DE)

97 The Sittingbourne and Kemsley Light Railway operates over some of the 2 foot 6 inch gauge lines of the Bowater Lloyds Pulp and Paper Mills in Kent, and by the time that company ceased to use its railway in 1969, the locomotives not required by the S&KLR were being disposed of to various societies around the country. *Excelsior* an 0-4-2ST built by Kerr Stuart in 1908 went to Whipsnade Zoo, and on Sunday, 17 September 1978, is working on the Whipsnade and Umfolozi Railway, taking visitors in the comparative safety of the train right through the rhino compound. (DE)

95

98

98 There are few towns in the world that can boast two
separate steam pleasure railways (Jenbach near Innsbruck in
Austria is one, having the Zillertalbahn and the Achenseebahn,
and Porthmadog is another with the well-established Festiniog
Railway, and the more recently founded Welsh Highland
Railway), but Llanberis has been in this happy position since
the attractions of the Snowdon Mountain Railway were
supplemented in the early seventies by the opening up of the
Llanberis Lake Railway, a very picturesque mile or so of 1 foot
11½ inch track along the water's edge. Motive power has
consisted mainly of ex-slate quarry locomotives (*Maid Marian*
was here after leaving Bressingham, and before going to Bala),
but the mainstay during the 1979 season was the 1922 Hunslet-
built 0-4-0ST *Dolbadarn,* shown on Thursday, 19 July at
Penllyn, about to return an early evening train to Llanberis.
(DE)

99 The only rack railway in Britian is the 2 foot 7½ inch
gauge line which runs up Snowdon, and this is worked by seven
0-4-2T Swiss-built locomotives; the first four from 1895-6, and
the rest from 1922-3, but all having that feature so common on
continental mountain locomotives, a sloping boiler, necessary to
keep the water in it level during the steep climb. This has
resulted in the nickname 'kneeling cows' being given to
locomotives with this feature, and on Easter Sunday, 1974, one
of the later batch (No. 8, *Eryri)* is being refuelled at Llanberis
in readiness for a journey to the summit at about 14.30hrs on a
dull April afternoon, following normal continental practice by
pushing a single coach to guard against runaways. (DE)

100 Not only is No. 390 (from the Zambezi Sawmills Railway)
the only (large) 4-8-0 locomotive in Britain, it is also the only 3
foot 6 inch gauge loco, and it is a wood-burner too! Africa's loss
is our gain, however, and thanks to artist and steam-enthusiast
David Shepherd who brought it over, this magnificent beast is
to be seen on a short length of track and in steam every so
often (like this occasion, with Ron Druce giving last-minute
instructions to the crew, on Sunday, 17 September 1978) in
Whipsnade Zoo. The 1896 locomotive was built in Glasgow by
Sharp Stewart. (DE)

A Few More Preserved Lines

101 Four or five miles of the old BR line between Peterborough and Northampton are operated by the Nene Valley Railway, and although they specialise mainly in foreign locomotives here, they do have others of note, especially a Standard 5 4-6-0 (a development of the Stanier Black Fives), and for a while the line played host to the ex-SR S15 4-6-0 No. 841 *Greene King,* shown on Sunday, 11 December 1977, leaving Wansford with a Santa Special. Towards the end of 1978, the locomotive moved to the NYMR. During the weekend of Saturday and Sunday, 23 and 24 September the NVR held a special event where no less than eight locomotives were in steam, and five of them were from countries other than Britain. The festivities were called 'Eurosteam '78', and three separate train-sets were used, hauled by various combinations of locomotives, both single- and double-headed. The first train of the day was hauled by the French 4-6-0 No. 3.628 of 1911 (actually built by Henschel in Germany!), . . .

102 . . . caught by the camera awaiting the off at Wansford at about 11.00hrs. (DE)

101

Some of the shorter lines, and lines with fewer locomotives at present, are included in this section, but, as can be seen, they are none the less interesting than their 'larger' counterparts, and certainly do not generally lack any of the scenic locations either. One or two of the lines have only recently come into operation, such as the Strathspey in 1978, for example, and geographically stretch from Scotland to Devon, passing through the Lake District, Norfolk and Kent on the way. The Nene Valley Railway with its predominance of foreign locomotives is included, as is the Torbay Steam Railway which played host to *Flying Scotsman* during the summer of 1973, and in fact there are examples of the locomotives of each of the 'Big Four' railway companies, with even a couple of industrials thrown in for good measure. Many of these railways have yet to fulfil their full potential with, for example, extensions planned and locomotives awaiting restoration, but all of this takes time and effort, both in effecting the work and in operating the various cash-raising schemes which often must be completed before the new ideas can even begin to be carried out. So time alone will tell whether or not another line with the scope of say, the Worth Valley or the Severn Valley, will eventually emerge.

105

103 Later in the afternoon of the weekend 23/34 September 1978, a rare combination returns from Orton Mere with yet another crowded train. The leading locomotive is a Danish F class 0-6-0T No. 656 of 1948, and the second is a DR (German) 2-6-2T No. 64.305 of 1934. (DE)

104 On Easter Sunday, 15 April 1979, the Swedish S class 2-6-2T No. 1178 of 1914 pauses briefly at Ferry Meadows with an afternoon train for Orton Mere. (DE)

105 During the afternoon of Sunday, 25 November 1973, Black Five 4-6-0 No. 5231 approaches Quorn with a train from Loughborough on the Main Line Steam Trust in Leicestershire. This sort of scene was sadly, soon to disappear when BR lifted one pair of rails a few years later. Before this happened, a really rare sight was to be seen on 13 December 1975 when the steam Sentinel Tank was used to move ex-GWR 4-6-0 No. 6990 *Witherslack Hall* . . . (DE)

106 . . . from Quorn to Loughborough after delivery from Barry scrapyard. (JHCS)

107 This is one of a pair of Norwegian 2-6-0 locomotives in the country. The other is on the Kent and East Sussex Railway, but here No. 377 *King Haakon* 7 nears Quorn at about 14.15hrs with a train from Loughborough on Saturday, 3 January 1976. (DE)

108 Not in working order, but nevertheless in pristine external condition, is the GCR 4-6-0 *Butler Henderson,* on loan from the National Collection, and on show in the loco shed at Loughborough on Sunday, 13 August 1978. (JHCS)

108

109 Amid the snows of 1 January 1979, N2 class 0-6-2T No. 4744 makes a splendid sight as it leaves Rothley for Loughborough. This Gresley-designed suburban tank engine was for some time on the K&WVR, but after moving here it has been extensively overhauled, and returned to service during 1978. (JHCS)

110 The Watercress line from Ropley to Alresford in Hampshire was re-opened shortly before this picture was taken on Sunday, 4 September 1977 of N class 2-6-0 No. 31874 and 'Austerity' 0-6-0ST *Errol Lonsdale* departing for Alresford. (JHCS)

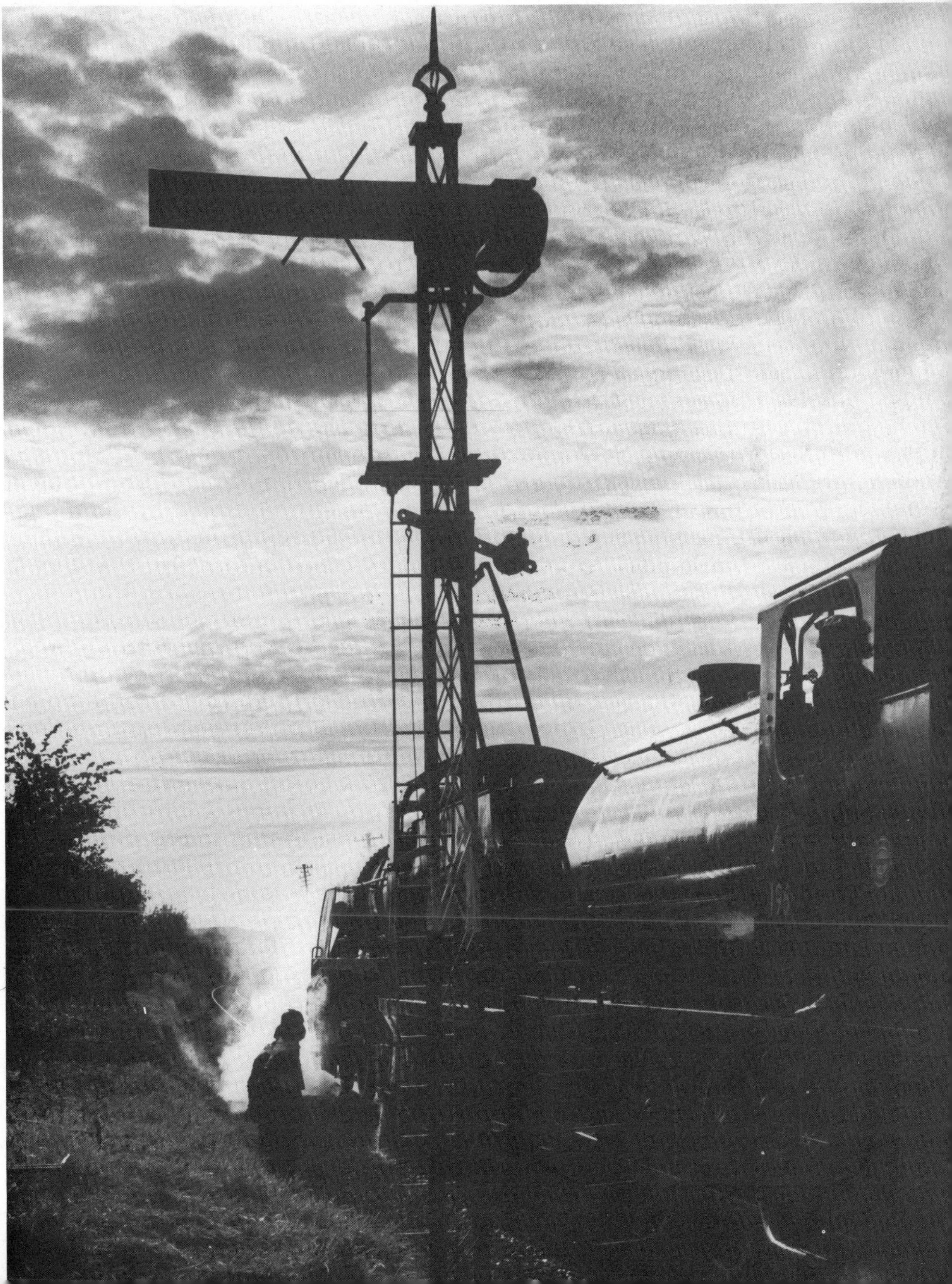

111 Rebuilt West Country class Pacific No. 34016 *Bodmin* undergoes the final stages of restoration in a polythene cocoon at Ropley as protection against the weather to enable the locomotive to return to service during 1979. It was thus protected on Saturday, 2 September 1978, whilst outside . . .

112 . . . on the line, N class No. 31874 is opened up a little with a train on the descent between Ropley and Alresford. (JHCS)

113 At the Dart Valley Railway's locomotive shed at Buckfastleigh, GWR Prairie Tank No. 4555 and 0-6-0 Pannier Tank No. 1638 receive the attention of the cleaning staff on Sunday, 1 June 1975. There are two Prairie Tanks at work in this part of the country, and the other one is . . .

114 . . . No. 4588, shuffling along here between Totnes and Buckfastleigh on Thursday, 23 June 1977. Note the authentic GWR headlamp code for a stopping passenger train; they always had to be different! (JHCS)

16

115 The nearby Torbay Steam Railway uses the larger locomotives of the stud set up by the original Dart Valley Railway administration, and on the occasion of the renaming ceremony of 4-6-0 No. 7827 *Lydham Manor*, a special double-header was run from Kingswear to Paignton on Saturday afternoon, 28 April 1973. Although it rained fairly persistently most of the time, this did not dampen the spirits of the hundreds of visitors and guests who witnessed the event. The second locomotive is the Prairie Tank No. 4555 which, along with other locomotives, shares its time between the TSR and the DVR. (DE)

116 During the summer of 1973, *Flying Scotsman* was at work on the Torbay Steam Railway but, unlike some other locomotives on the line, faced *down* to the River Dart. Consequently, for the return to Paignton, it had to run tender-first as it is shown doing on Saturday afternoon, 15 September. More tender-first working is shown on Sunday, 21 May 1975, when *Lydham Manor* climbs from Greenway Tunnel . . . (DE)

117 . . . towards Churston and Paignton. A new turntable on the line allows much easier turning than before when this had to be done via BR. (JHCS)

117

118 During the Silver Jubilee celebrations in 1977, the Lakeside and Haverthwaite Railway used the Fairburn 2-6-4T No. 2085 on some of its services, and on 1 June it runs round its train between the tunnels at Haverthwaite. (JHCS)

119 A new line to open in 1978 was the Strathspey which runs from Aviemore to Boat of Garten, and on August Bank Holiday that year, Ivatt class 2 2-6-0 No. 46464 of 1950, not yet fully lined out, rests between turns at Aviemore. (JHCS)

120 The North Norfolk Railway runs between Sheringham and Weybourne, and throughout its short length, is never very far fom the sea. Most of the locomotives on stock are ex-industrials most admirably employed, but of particular note is the LNER 4-6-0 B12 No. 61572 of 1928, awaiting restoration on Sunday, 23 October 1977. (DE)

121 Also on Sunday, 23 October 1977 the GER J15 0-6-0 No. 564 hauls a five-coach train out of Sheringham, newly restored and working its first public passenger train in this condition. (DE)

122 No. 3 *Bodiam* is one of the original 0-6-0T 'Terrier' class locomotives designed by William Stroudley in 1872, and is once again at work on the Kent & East Sussex Railway where, on Saturday, 8 June 1974, it easily lifts its light load from Rolvenden up the incline towards Tenterden. (DE)

Centres Not Concerned with Steam on British Rail

Many locations up and down the country do not have a permanent connection with British Rail, and consequently do not provide locomotives to haul main-line specials, even though in some cases they would be perfectly capable of so doing. It is some of these centres that are featured in this chapter and lack of main-line accessibility in no way implies lack of other facilities or achievements, as a glance at some of the following photographs shows. At Bressingham, for example, there are locomotives of the *Royal Scot, Coronation* and *Britannia* classes being beautifully restored, maintained and steamed, all within the confines of the gardens, and at Butterley (Derbyshire) and Beamish (Co. Durham), the achievements of two

local government-sponsored schemes amply demonstrate how worthwhile such schemes can be. Long-term hopes and aspirations include such aims as the running of steam-hauled trains from Quainton to Aylesbury, and the Midland Railway Trust at Butterley to form the base of a new preserved line to Pye Bridge. And who knows where it will all end? The Waverley Route (Carlisle — Edinburgh) and the Somerset and Dorset line (Bath — Bournemouth) may be gone forever, but steam is returning to Swanage, and is already a reality in two other parts of Somerset (Cranmore and Minehead), so the future looks very bright indeed. Thank goodness!

123

123 Quainton Road depot on the old GCR near Aylesbury houses a truly remarkable collection of locomotives ranging downwards in size from a 'King' to various small industrials, including one of the unusual Aveling & Porter geared 0-4-0WTs, which look more like steamrollers than railway engines! Many of the locomotives are being painstakingly restored to working-order by hard pressed (and hard-up!) volunteers, but something is usually to be found in steam here during summer weekends, and often at other times too. During the Easter holiday of 1970, the society proudly shows off one of its latest acquisitions, the GWR 0-6-0PT No. 7715 which had recently arrived from its last owners, London Transport, bearing the number L99. The following year, on Sunday, 26 September crew-training takes place using . . .

124 . . . the Beattie 2-4-0WT of 1874, and . . .

125 . . . on Easter Monday, 1975, the public is being treated to steam-hauled rides using *Coventry No. 1*, the North British built 0-6-0T of 1939. (DE)

125

126 Representative of the many military railway centres that were once active in Britain, Long Marston, near Stratford on Avon, held an Open Day on Saturday, 29 September 1973. The passengers who arrived from Didcot, were entertained by being steam-hauled by No. 6998 *Burton Agnes Hall*. The army's 'star attraction' was the 1953 Hunslet-built 0-6-0ST No. 98, *Royal Engineer*, and although the order of the day seemed to be rain most of the time, the sun did occasionally break through. The 'Austerity' sends smoke skywards at the start of one of its trips round the camp. (DE)

127 A temporary but, of course, very large steam-centre was set up in August 1975 at Shildon in connection with the Rail 150 celebrations. A small fraction of the motive-power present can be seen here, including Pacifics *Flying Scotsman* and *Clan Line*, 4-6-0s *Leander* and *Greene King*, and the Midland Compound, amongst others. Note, top left, the coal in the bunker of *Fenchurch*; it has been white-washed for the occasion! And not an RSM in sight, either! (JHCS)

128 As yet still a steam-centre, but in years to come hopefully the hub of a very interesting preserved line is that at Butterley, on the line between Ambergate and Pye Bridge, Derbyshire. Under restoration here on Sunday, 13 August 1978, is Caprotti class 5 4-6-0 No. 73129, whilst already in steamable condition is . . .

129 . . . the 1897 MR 'Spinner' 4-2-2 No. 673, resting in the loco shed the same day. (JHCS)

129

130 At Beamish, Co. Durham, a special industrial museum has been set up on an outdoor site, and one of the features is a complete steam-worked railway consisting of this 1889 NER J21 class 0-6-0 Gateshead-built locomotive, matching rolling-stock from the same company, and even station buildings and signalling recovered from the old NER station at Rowley. On Saturday, 26 August 1978, No. 876 (ex-BR No. 65033) gently brews up before setting off on a trip to the other end of the line 600 yards away where . . .

131 . . . it passes an ancient and derelict clerestory coach.
(JHCS)

132

100

133

134

132 A fine collection of locomotives both large and small exists at Bressingham near Diss in Norfolk, and it is a pity that, due to there being no connection with BR, we are unlikely to see any of these magnificent machines at work on steam specials in years to come. But we can, and do, admire them here, as on Sunday, 4 July 1971, when the last steam locomotive to receive a general overhaul by BR, the Britannia class Pacific No. 70013, *Oliver Cromwell*, moves amongst the trees giving footplate rides to eager visitors, and on Sunday, 3 June 1973 . . .

133 . . . LMS 4-6-0 No. 6100 *Royal Scot* darkens the sky outside the museum buildings. Locomotives are steamed here on Sundays and Thursdays throughout the 'season', and it is on Thursday, 29 May 1975 that . . . (DE)

134 . . . soon after its arrival from France, the huge SNCF 141R 2-8-2 locomotive makes such an impressive sight on its short length of demonstration track. A month or so later, . . .

135 ... on 19 June the prototype Stanier 3 cylinder 2-6-4T No. 2500 prepares to give footplate rides, while after about another month ...

136 ... on Sunday, 20 July the pride of Bressingham, Coronation class Pacific No. 6233 *Duchess of Sutherland* gladdens the eye with its superlative appearance. (JHCS)

137 In 1969, *Stowe* was at Beaulieu. Built at Eastleigh in 1934, this 4-4-0 Schools class locomotive was withdrawn from service in 1962, and later put on display at Lord Montagu's Motor Museum, along with 3 Pullman coaches where it quietly rests on Saturday, 28 June. The collection was later dispersed, and the locomotive has gone to Cranmore where it is now to be seen alongside David Shepherd's other fine 'giants' *Black Prince* and *The Green Knight*. (DE)

137

The British Rail Connected Centres

138 On 14 September 1969, one of the first Open Days at Didcot engine shed takes place, and 0-4-2T No. 1466 is working an auto-train up and down a demonstration track. The depot plays host to visiting locomotives from time to time, and, . . . (JHCS)

139 . . . on Saturday, 10 June 1972, the only existing example of a Peppercorn Pacific, the 1948 built A2 class No. 532 *Blue Peter* is much admired as it posed peacefully in the sunshine. (DE)

138

Most of the centres with main-line connections are ex-British Rail motive power depots (Hereford being a notable exception), and it is from here and places such as York, Carnforth and Didcot that the locomotives hauling the enthusiasts' specials which have become such a popular part of the preservation movement in recent years come. These sites also double as museums for static exhibits, besides offering facilities for running repairs and restoration to the very high standards required for main-line running. The depot at Hereford is unusual in that it is on the premises of a private firm, H. P. Bulmer Ltd., the cider-makers, whose managing director Mr Peter Prior so actively supports the steam preservation programme; and at Dinting, what was in the days of steam but a small sub-depot, is today a first-class repair and maintenance centre from where one

locomotive, *Scots Guardsman,* has already been used hauling specials on the main line after complete restoration on the premises, and more are to follow. The representative museum at Dinting often includes locomotives loaned by the National Railway Museum at York (this honour is not granted lightly), and during 1978, the two famous pacifics *Blue Peter* and *Bittern* arrived to augment an already interesting collection, putting this Derbyshire depot amongst the forefront of our active museums. Tyseley too utilises its well-equipped workshops to keep *Clun Castle* a regular performer on the main line, and uses its turntable, watering and coaling facilities to service visiting locomotives on steam tours from Didcot. We are indeed fortunate in this country that so much has been saved for future generations to value before it is too late.

139

140 On Sunday, 16 April 1978, one of Didcot's 'main-line' locomotives, 4-6-0 No. 5900 *Hinderton Hall* steams along the demonstration track, passing two of the depot's locomotives undergoing restoration, 2-8-2T No. 7202, and the 0-6-0 Pannier Tank. Recently arrived Battle of Britain class Pacific *Winston Churchill*, . . .

141 . . . having been in store since hauling the train involved in Sir Winston's funeral in 1965, is proudly shown off, also on 16 April, which was one of the occasions when *Clun Castle* worked a special here from Tyseley. The volunteer cleaners . . .

142 . . . demonstrate just how much 'foreign matter' can accumulate on a steam locomotive during such a short trip! (JHCS)

142

143 As well as the stud of ex-BR locomotives, Carnforth has two foreign Pacific locomotives. Here we see the SNCF 231 K 22 moving off the ash-pits with drain-cocks open on Easter Sunday, 18 April 1976. (JHCS)

144 The other Carnforth foreign Pacific is the DB (West German) oil-burning class 012 No. 012 104-6 moving massively forward on Saturday, 19 June of the same year. Steamtown, as the railway museum at Carnforth is known, is at the centre of steam operations on BR in the north west, many of BR's own steam specials to Sellafield and the SLOA specials on the Settle & Carlisle line being powered by locomotives from here. (JHCS)

143

145

145 During 1978, the two most regular performers between Sellafield and Skipton were the big Pacifics, *Flying Scotsman* and *Sir Nigel Gresley,* caught being prepared for the day's outings on the morning of Tuesday, 29 August, whilst on Saturday, 16 of the next month, another Pacific, No. 35028 . . .

146 . . . *Clan Line* exchanges greetings with 231 K 22 after working in a special from Leeds. The 'Golden Arrow' insignia is particularly appropriate since both locomotives in their day have worked their own sections of this well-known boat-train between London and Paris. (JHCS)

144

146

147 Having been based all its life since restoration at Dinting, Stanier 4-6-0 No. 5690 *Leander* changed owners and had to leave there early in 1979, so on Saturday, 24 February it worked a rail-tour via Sheffield, York and Leeds to arrive after dark at Carnforth. There was nothing for it but to get out the tripod and photograph it having its fire thrown at about 20.00hrs that evening. (DE)

148 The first centre to be involved with steam running on BR since the 1968 'ban' was that at Hereford, in Bulmer's sidings, and the locomotive used was the GWR 4-6-0 No. 6000 *King George V*, seen here entering the depot soon after the completion of its restoration. A stranger at Bulmer's on Saturday, 4 October 1975 was . . . (JHCS)

148

149 . . . the LMS 4-6-0 locomotive *Leander,* being serviced before returning a special to Chester, and seen in company with the 0-6-0PT No. 5786 and *King George V,* most unusually on public display without the famous bell on the front buffer-beam. (DE)

150 On Sunday, 16 June 1978, there was an Open Day held in Doncaster Works when, amongst others, some of the locomotives from the National Railway Museum, York, were put on display, and included the record-breaking A4 Pacific *Mallard* and the 1870 Stirling Single No. 1. Just as the NRM will, on occasion, lend locomotives to suitable organisations (*Evening Star* on the KWVR (pics 27 & 28) is an example of this), so the museum will also play host to non-NRM locomotives when the need arises, and the Hull-based Black Five 4-6-0 No. 5305 has spent a good deal of its time at York, and worked many rail-tours since first re-entering service after restoration in 1977. During the early hours of Saturday, 8 April 1978, it is steamed outside the museum for just such a tour;

151

152 Of the four Jubilee class locomotives still in existence, two *Bahamas* and *Leander* were together at Dinting until they were parted early in 1979 when *Leander* moved to Carnforth. The third, *Kolhapur*, is at Tyseley where it is still to be available for main-line excursions, and the fourth, *Galatea* is rusting away at Barry. But on 16 June 1974 No. 5690 *Leander* was very much a part of the attractions at Dinting as the beautiful red locomotive demonstrates its mobility for the benefit of visitors. (JHCS)

153 On Saturday, 11 November 1978, the Royal Scot class 4-6-0 locomotive No. 6115 *Scots Guardsman* sits with steam to spare in the early morning sunshine all ready to work a special train through to York. (JHCS)

154 A very sad day at Dinting was 24 February 1979 for that was the day when *Leander* said goodbye after so many happy and successful years at the Derbyshire depot, but at about 08.30hrs, it fits in perfectly between *Scots Guardsman* and *Bahamas* . . . and receives last attentions before making its final and very moving departure. (DE)

157

155 The site of the old motive power depot at Tyseley in Birmingham forms the Tyseley Steam Centre, and this has been open since 1970 when on 17 May, an Open Day was held. Various of their own and visiting locomotives were on show, and there were even steam-hauled rides to be enjoyed along a few hundred yeards of track with a train four-coaches long and a locomotive on each end! 4-6-0 class 5 No. 5428 *Eric Treacy* handles the return-to-base leg, whilst . . .

156 . . . *Kolhapur,* the Jubilee class locomotive, moves the joyous passengers outwards. (JHCS)

157 One of the visitors at the Tyseley Steam Centre on 17 May 1970 was Princess Royal class Pacific No. 6201 *Princess Elizabeth* which shows off its classic lines during a brief stay away from its home of that time, Ashchurch near Tewkesbury. (JHCS)

158 Another visitor at the Open Day, 1970 at Tyseley Steam Centre was the Stanier 2-8-0 8F locomotive from the Severn Valley Railway which is also much admired. By 1978, however, visiting locomotives . . .

159 . . . are confined to those which work in to the depot with special trains, as on 15 October, when 7808 *Cookham Manor* (left) and *Hinderton Hall* are each turned on the turntable ready to double-head the Great Western Society's vintage train back to Didcot. The weather, often so unkind when steam is being used, was its usual dreadful self this day, and the return train departed for home in the deepening gloom. (JHCS)

160 Although based in a storage shed at Markinch, Fife, A4 Pacific No. 60009 *Union of South Africa* has received its more major repairs at Haymarket motive power depot, Edinburgh, and on Friday, 23 September 1977, returns to accompany a replica of *Locomotion* at an Open Day. (JHCS)

158

159

Index